Special Days

Family Vacations

by Heather Adamson

Amicus Readers are published by Amicus
P.O. Box 1329, Mankato, Minnesota 56002

Printed in the United States of America at Corporate Graphics, North Mankato, Minnesota.

Library of Congress Cataloging-in-Publication Data
Adamson, Heather, 1974-
Family vacations / by Heather Adamson.
p. cm. -- (Amicus readers. Special days)
Includes index.
Summary: "Describes different ways people spend family vacations. Includes simple craft"--Provided by publisher.
ISBN 978-1-60753-029-9 (library binding)
1. Family vacations--Juvenile literature. I. Title.
GV182.8.A27 2011
790.1'91--dc22

2010000836

Series Editor	Rebecca Glaser
Series Designer	Emily Brown
Book Designer	Heather Dreisbach
Photo Researcher	Heather Dreisbach

Photo Credits
Andresr/iStockphoto, 5, 21 (b); Chet Mitchell/iStockphoto, 6, 21 (t); danilovi/iStockphoto, 3, 20–24 (travel collage); G. Palmer/Alamy, 17; Jose Luis Pelaez/Getty Images, cover; Orange Line Media/Shutterstock, 12, 20 (t); Photodisc, 11, 15, 20 (m, b); Pierre Jacques/Getty Images, 8, 9, 20 (b); Racheal Grazias/Shutterstock, 16, 21 (m); Robert Warren/Getty Images, 19; Stockbyte, 1, 7; Vladimir Mucibabic/iStockphoto, 13

1225
42010

10 9 8 7 6 5 4 3 2 1

Table of Contents

Vacations with Your Family 6

Picture Glossary 20

Make a Memory Box 22

Ideas for Parents and Teachers 23

Index and Web Sites 24

Many families take vacations.

They do something different from school or work.

They do something special together.

Lana's family went fishing by a stream.

She caught minnows with a net.

Jake hiked with his dad for a day on his vacation.

They used hiking poles on the rough, steep ground.

hiking pole

Adam spent his vacation with his cousins.

They went swimming every day.

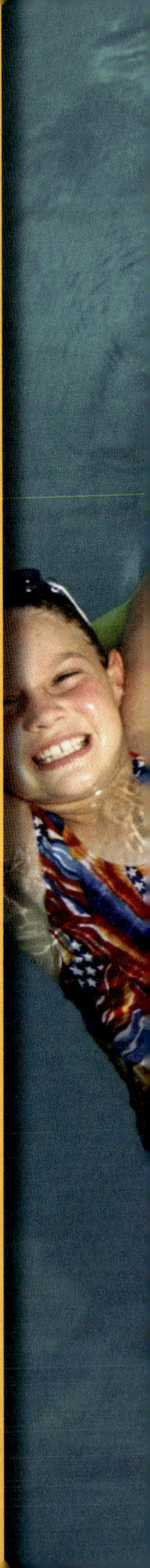

Hakim's family stayed home for their vacation.

They played games. His grandpa was the best at checkers.

On their vacation, Beth and her friends marched in the city parade.

They wore costumes. They made everyone smile.

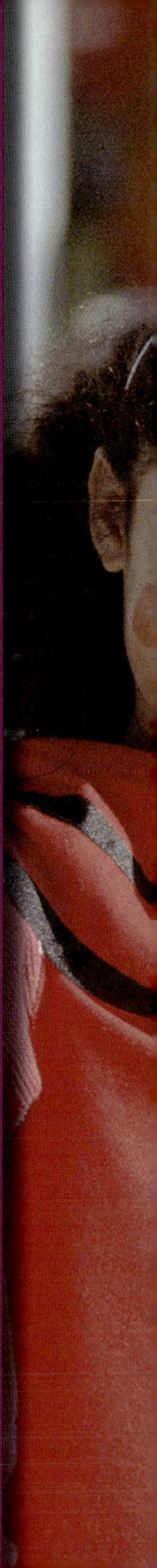

Kali and her family went to an amusement park.

They rode a roller coaster.

roller coaster

No matter what you do, family vacations are a great time.

It's always fun—until it's time for it to end!

Picture Glossary

checkers

a game for two people with 12 round pieces each, played on a board marked with squares of alternating colors

costume

an outfit or clothes that make you look like something else

hiking pole

pole used to help keep balanced while walking or hiking through mountains

minnow net

a net with very small holes used to catch tiny fish called minnows

roller coaster

an amusement park ride where a train of cars goes very fast over a track that rises, falls, and curves

vacation

a break from regular schedule; people often take trips on their vacations.

Make a Memory Box

Supplies:

- Small box with lid
- String
- Small notebook
- Pencil

1. Have a parent poke holes on each side of the box. Tie the string to them to make a handle. Put your notebook and pencil in the box.
2. Carry your memory box with you. On your vacation, collect items to remind you of where you went.
3. Write or draw a story about each place you visit.
4. When you get home, show people the things in your memory box. Tell them about your vacation.

Ideas for Parents and Teachers

Special Days, an Amicus Readers Level 1 series, gives children practice reading about celebrations they will likely encounter. The picture glossary reinforces new vocabulary. The activities give children a chance to apply what they have learned. Use the ideas listed below to help children get even more out of their reading experience.

Before Reading:

- Ask children to tell about a time when they went on vacation.
- Look at the picture glossary. Tell children to watch for the words while reading.

Read the Book:

- Read the book to the children or have them read independently.
- Show children how to use the photo labels and picture glossary to help them read new words.

After Reading:

- Ask children how vacations in the book were the same as or different from what they have done on vacation.
- Ask children to draw pictures and write down what they did on vacation.
- Talk about what makes a vacation special. What is different on a vacation day from a regular day?

Index

amusement parks 16
checkers 12
costumes 14
cousins 10
fishing 6
hiking 8
parades 14
playing games 12
roller coasters 16
staying home 12
swimming 10

Web Sites

Family Travel Advice—Travel Activities and Checklists
http://www.nickjr.com/family-trips/travel-activities-checklists/

On the Road Games
http://familyfun.go.com/vacations/on-the-road-games/

U.S. State Maps—Free Printable Maps
http://www.yourchildlearns.com/us-state-maps.htm

Vacation Memory Book
http://www.enchantedlearning.com/crafts/books/vacationmemory/